HOW TO TURN YOUR JOB INTO
A HIGH PAYING POSITION

HAROLD HERRING
President, Debt Free Army

The Debt Free Army
Post Office Box 900000, Fort Worth, TX 76161

How To Turn Your Job Into A High Paying Position
by Harold Herring

ISBN 0-9763668-090000

Copyright © 2004 by The Debt Free Army
Fort Worth, Texas

Debt Free Army, Post Office Box 900000, Fort Worth, TX 76161
www.debtfreearmy.org

A Personal Word

I would like to dedicate this book to John and Patricia Avanzini. John Avanzini, known to millions of television viewers as Brother John, is the most widely-published author and teacher on the subject of biblical economics and debt-free living.

But to me, Brother John is my friend, a spiritual father and the most unassuming leader I've ever met. God used Brother John at a defining moment in my life to move me out of my comfort zone... to open my eyes to revelation in the Word so that I could join him in helping to get the Body of Christ out of debt.

I also want to honor Sister Pat who has always been right by Brother John's side helping him spread the message of financial freedom. A sought-after preacher in her own right, Sister Pat was the Founding Pastor of International Faith Center, my home church for seven years.

Finally, I want to honor the greatest wife any man could ever have. My "fine" wife, Bev, is the epitome of a Proverbs 31 woman who kept faith in me even when it wasn't easy. She is editor of the Debt Free Living magazine, my co-laborer, but most of all, she's my best friend.

To Bev, I'd say, "the best is yet to come."

WHY SHOULD YOU READ THIS BOOK?

Almost every day there seems to be another report of employee layoffs, company sell outs, work slow downs and jobs going overseas. And with these reports comes the heart-breaking stories of lives being interrupted by financial circumstances beyond their control.

People are losing their life-savings, marriages, homes and everything they've worked so hard to achieve simply because of "the way the economy is."

But here's the good news…

At a time when people are losing their jobs, you can keep yours and even get promoted! However, if you're uninformed you too might be among those who are struggling just to get by.

The scripture is quite clear when it says it rains on the just and the wicked alike (Matthew 5:45). God moves with an even hand across the earth with those who do not know the inside Bible truth of God's plan for His children. With a proper understanding and the right introduction, there is a way you can insulate yourself from losing your job and even turn it into a HIGH PAYING POSITION.

I can show you a proven principle in the scriptures that explains how you can give your job to the Lord, and He will add a supernatural dimension to it… one that will put your job into a protected place that the world cannot touch.

3

In addition, in the pages of this book you will learn practical and proven approaches to strengthen your value as an employee. Strategies that will increase your worth as an employee and put you in line for a HIGH PAYING POSITION.

This book contains up-to-the-minute information on how to protect your job from the economic realities of today's turbulent world and to ensure that you receive what's rightfully promised to you from the Word of God.

I suggest that you read this book with a pen in your hand so you don't miss one nugget in HOW TO TURN YOUR JOB INTO A HIGH PAYING POSITION. Get ready, for you are on the threshold of turning even a mundane job into a position of substantial status.

HAROLD HERRING
President and Co-Founder, Debt Free Army

CHAPTER 1

FIRST THINGS FIRST

In the book of Exodus, there is an almost hidden revelation folded into the first twenty verses of the fourth chapter, a picture in type of a person's employment being given to the Lord.

You might be out there today as a bricklayer, a bank teller, working in an office somewhere, or you might own your own business. But if you want something better than what you have, pay attention. God took Moses from a very ho-hum job of a shepherd on the backside of the desert and turned him into the most powerful man of his time in the land of Egypt, placing him in stature above Pharaoh himself. Let me show you what your Bible says about this.

"And the LORD said unto [Moses], What is that in thine hand? And he said, A rod."

Exodus 4:2

Moses answered God by telling Him it's a shepherd's rod. Now the shepherd's rod represented Moses' vocation. He was a common sheepherder wandering in the desert taking care of a group of sheep that were not even his own. They belonged to his father-in-law. But without even a moment's hesitation Moses gave the rod to God. Now remember this rod symbolized his secular employment, however something exciting is about to happen because we all know that whatsoever God touches is going to take on Kingdom significance.

"...thou shalt take this rod in thine hand, wherewith thou shalt do signs."

Exodus 4:17

Just a few minutes earlier Moses' job (vocation) was under his control, however, now the Lord controlled Moses' job (rod). Notice that Moses' shepherd's rod was now in God's control as God gave it back to Moses. Now here's the powerful part of all this. Not only did God give Moses control over the now anointed shepherd's rod but God added His mighty power to it.

"And Moses took his wife and his sons, and set them upon an ass, and he returned to the land of Egypt: and Moses took the rod of God in his hand."

Exodus 4:20

Keep in mind that when Moses started out, it was his shepherd's rod. Then he put his shepherd's rod (a symbol of the way he made his living) into the Lord's hand, and when the Lord gave it back into Moses' hand, it was no longer just a shepherd's rod, it became "the rod of God."

Now watch God's Holy Word as He tells us exactly what happened to Moses' shepherd's rod after it became the rod of God.

"...Be sure to take your rod along so that you can perform the miracles I have shown you."

Exodus 4:17 TLB

It became a miracle working rod in Moses' hands. Now I can hear you saying, "Well, that was Moses and God, not me." So I would ask you, "Why would God want you to read these verses? Why didn't

He just skip this part unless He wanted you to understand the principle behind what happened here?"

Before Moses handed over his vocation to God he was in charge of his own destiny. He was the sole proprietor of his sheepherder business. That is until God showed him how he could make his job an effective part of God's Kingdom business.

Make no mistake about it. This very day you can make that same decision. Instead of giving to God, put yourself in the position of someone who manages the assets of God.

Believe me. This is a God principle that works. People who have put this principle into practice have come to me and said since they've given their job to God and become stewards for Him, almost without exception, they have started seeing supernatural things happening in their lives. It's not uncommon to hear that co-workers with more seniority than they had have been let go and yet they kept their job.

If you follow the example of Moses' release and take your job out of your hands and put it in God's hands, you will immediately begin to see the power and protection God brings over it. Please know that we're not talking small potatoes here. That simple shepherd's rod went before the nation of Israel in a mighty deliverance.

As you place your job into God's hands and allow it to become "God's job," He will multiply finances, influence and advancement in the same way He did for Moses. When your job is "God's job," it will be up to Him to see to it that you don't get laid off. And if you do get laid off, in a short time you'll have a better job than you had before.

Read Ecclesiastes 5:18 very carefully.

"Behold that which I have seen: it is good and comely for one to eat and to drink, and to enjoy the good of all his labour that he taketh under the sun all the days of his life, which God giveth him: for it is his portion."

You and your job can become fire proof, lay-off proof, even pink-slip proof if you give your job to God and let Him take over as the new manager/owner of your talents and skills. With His help you can turn your job into a HIGH PAYING POSITION. Praise the Lord!!

Meditate on this powerful saying, "Little becomes much when God is in it."

"In order to succeed you must know what you are doing, like what you are doing, and believe in what you are doing."

Will Rogers

Who's the boss?

If I were to ask ten people, including believers, who they work for, nine out of the ten would give the wrong answer. They might say... American Airlines, IBM, General Motors, the Federal Government, Mom and Pop's Diner down the street. The real truth is that no matter where you work, the company only writes your check. The truth you must know to get ahead and stay ahead is that you really work for God.

"...rendering service [to your employer] with good will as to the Lord and not to men..."

Ephesians 6:7 Paraphrased

That's right. You should do EVERYTHING, and that includes your job, as if you were the Lord's employee. When you understand the principle of performing your assigned responsibilities as unto the Lord and not to men, you immediately add an extra dimension of powerful success and advancement to whatever vocation you might be involved in. This mindset will immediately increase the value you place on the things that you do for your employer. At the same time, your position of employment will take on a much higher level of value.

There is a powerful principle of increase behind the mindset of being the Lord's employee. If you're doing your job as unto the Lord, there will be a more valuable standard of excellence that will guide your effectiveness as well as your enthusiasm for your job. Do you see how this alone can be an asset?

Not long ago it was popular to wear a bracelet that said, "WWJD" (What Would Jesus Do?). That is the same question you must answer every day on your job. **What would you do differently on your job if you knew that Jesus would be evaluating your performance?**

Truthfully, He is. The scripture is quite clear. We should do "EVERYTHING" as unto the Lord.

The first step to increasing your value as an employee/employer is to determine who's the boss.

"Heavenly Father, I ask in the name of Jesus, that you help the reader of these words to fully understand 'Who's the Boss.' I also ask that you give him or her a new appreciation for their employer. Please give them a heartfelt desire to pray for their employer, to lift them up each day. In the strong name of Jesus. Amen."

WORKING THE WORD TODAY

"God bless you for your prayers. I was amazed on September 16th, when the person you prayed for me to have favor with called me to the front office and offered me a wonderful new job. I will be working in quality control and my salary increased to $1,550 per month take home pay. I have a promise of a raise in January. God bless you. Thank you for your wonderful work."

CANDY, CALYPSO, NC

CHAPTER 2

WORK IS A GIFT FROM GOD

"...to rejoice in [your] labour; this is the gift of God."
Ecclesiastes 5:19

Statistics tell us that seventy percent of the labor force is working on the wrong job. This means the gifts and talents God placed within you could very possibly be overlooked or under-used.

When you learn to treat your work as a valuable gift from God, you will become a problem solver in the midst of a work force that is a constant problem to their employers.

Here are three truths about your job/vocation:

First, work is a gift God gives to you personally. It is provided to bless you and your loved ones, not to burden you or bring you down. It helps you discover and develop the dominant qualities in your life. It exposes you to other people and allows you to increase your communication skills. Work allows you to both speak and listen to others. Anytime you become a better communicator, your chances of winning others support immediately increases.

Second, your work is a gift from God for others around you. When others see you do your part and more, it inspires them to also become a better employee, thereby maximizing their potential. Your work done properly, with a proper attitude creates life, movement, progress and energy.

Third, your work is a gift of God to your family. The way you work becomes the example your family will follow. My parents taught me an incredible work ethic growing up. They didn't believe that "work" was a four-letter word scrawled on a bathroom wall. I was taught the value of work and the reward of seeing a job well done. What price can you put on the satisfaction of knowing you've done your best?

For instance, my Mom and Dad earned the money to make the down payment on their first business by collecting scrap metal and cans in the woods surrounding our country home. At the time Mom and Dad were sharecroppers on another man's land. We lived nearly a mile off the main highway up in the fields with no electricity and no running water.

When Mom and Dad bought the grocery store/service station we moved to the big city of LaGrange, North Carolina, population: 2,000 at the time.

From the time my Dad moved to the "big city" I never saw him go to work without wearing a white shirt and tie. Dad wore that clean, neatly pressed, white shirt and tie because he was proud to be the owner of his own business. He also understood that you dress for the job you want, not the one that you have.

He saw work and his ability to do it as a gift from God. Dad knew that a job provides the financial means through which a person can take care of their family's needs. Remember, it was God who gave Adam a direct command to take dominion and become productive. You must never lose sight of the fact that in our contemporary society, without your job, everything important to you is immediately placed in jeopardy.

CHAPTER 3

L OVE WHAT YOU DO AND DO WHAT YOU LOVE

"If you love your work, you'll be out there every day trying to do it the best you possibly can, and pretty soon everybody around will catch the passion from you—like a fever."

Sam Walton
Founder of Wal-Mart

Pause for a moment and think of what you would like most to do with the rest of your life. You might say, "I'm waiting for God to show me." Let me let you in on a little secret. Whatever your passion is will most likely be related to the vocation that God would have you to be employed at. For instance, if you love the outdoors, you aren't going to be happy as a bookkeeper. And a bookkeeper isn't going to be happy in an outdoors job. If your vocation is the one God has for you, it will be obvious to you. BUT, you must ALWAYS be faithful at what you're doing RIGHT NOW. He would expect no less from you, His faithful servant.

What do you like to talk about most? If you are like most people, you talk about three things:

1. The things you hate:

_____

_____

_____

13

2. The things you love:

_____

_____

_____

3. The things you fear:

_____

_____

_____

Keep adding to your lists for the next several days. I think you will be surprised to find where your focus lies.

"The way to change your destiny is to change what you do each day."

1. What books do you read?

_____

_____

_____

2. What magazines do you subscribe to?

_____

_____

_____

3. What type of movies and television programs do you watch?

_____

_____

_____

IF YOU COULD DO ANYTHING IN THE WORLD, KNOWING THAT YOU COULD NOT POSSIBLY FAIL, WHAT WOULD YOU CHOOSE TO DO?

1. What would you tell God that you wanted to do? Write down your ideas.

_____

_____

_____

_____

2. What would you want others to say about your life when you have gone on to meet the Lord? How will your obituary read? Write it down the way it would read if you died today.

_____

_____

_____

_____

_____

3. Now take a couple of minutes and write out the way you'd really like for your obituary to read.

_____

_____

_____

_____

_____

CHAPTER 4

L EARN EVERYTHING POSSIBLE ABOUT YOUR JOB ➤

"A wise man will hear, and will increase learning."
Proverbs 1:5

Paul wrote to young Timothy, ". . .**give attendance to reading**..." (1 Tim 4:13) and, "**Study to show thyself approved... a workman that needeth not to be ashamed**..." (2 Tim 2:15).

Hosea proclaimed "**My people are destroyed (bound) for lack of knowledge**" (Hosea 4:6). It is interesting that Hosea did not say that Satan would destroy you. He says that ignorance would destroy you. Satan just helps you enjoy staying ignorant.

The right information will not only promote you, it will motivate you and give you confidence.

"...through knowledge shall the just be delivered."
Proverbs 11:9

The difference between success and just getting by is usually due to three forces.

1. **Information** The successful person knows something that others have not yet discovered or cared to pursue. They find time to enjoy good books or tapes that will prepare and provoke them to stretch beyond their previous level of achievement. This works for

16

successful people and it will most surely WORK FOR YOU.

With a new passion for acquiring knowledge, what books and tapes should be on your priority list?

_____

_____

_____

_____

2. <u>**Motivation**</u> You must start clearly defining projects and goals that lie before you. See to it that you work with real enthusiasm in whatever you're doing. Here are two power thoughts to help you understand more clearly what enthusiasm really means. The last four letters of the word "enthusiasm" are "iasm" which stand for "I am sold myself." The word "enthusiasm" literally means "God within." When you can allow the greater one within you to stir your greatest desire for excellence, you will have all the motivation you need.

What is your motivation? What are your projects and goals? Be specific.

_____

_____

_____

_____

"Every job is a self-portrait of the person who did it."
Zig Ziglar

3. <u>**Associations**</u> A successful person knows how to build a bridge instead of a barrier. You're influenced by people you associate with. Make it a blessing. Spend your time with those who can encourage, edify, lift you up, build you up and sincerely want you to be all that God created you to be.

In Genesis 39:5, the scripture says "... the Egyptian [Potiphar] was blessed because Joseph was in his house." In Genesis 30:27, Laban said to Jacob, "... I have learned by experience that God blessed me for your sake."

So spend your time with people who can challenge you to even greater levels of accomplishment. Create a list of people with whom you like to associate with and why.

_____

_____

_____

_____

Now create a list of people that you would like to be associated with. People who can help you get where God wants you to be on your job.

_____

_____

_____

_____

WORKING THE WORD TODAY

During my annual performance review I was overwhelmed with blessings. I was given a Performance Award including $1,025 on my next check and my boss offered me a Divisional Manager position sixteen months away. It was the one I was praying for."

JOHN, SEAL BEACH, CA

CHAPTER 5

D ON'T WASTE YOUR TIME OR ANYBODY ELSE'S

"Waste your money and you're only out of money, but waste your time and you've lost part of your life."

Anonymous

If I were to ask if you have ever stolen from your employer you would probably say, "Absolutely not." In fact, you might even be offended by the question. My purpose is not to offend you but to provoke you to good works (Hebrews 10:24).

How does a person steal from an employer and not even notice that they're doing it?

1. Come to work five minutes late
2. Spend the first 20 minutes at the coffee machine
3. Make unnecessary trips to the water cooler
4. Surf the internet for personal pleasure or personal business
5. Chat with workers instead of taking care of business
6. Make lengthy personal phone calls
7. Play games on the computer
8. Run errands on company time
9. Stretch break time
10. Leave early for lunch
11. Come back late from lunch
12. Leave work five minutes early

Let me put this in a proper perspective. If you come to work five minutes late and leave five minutes early each day, that would represent a total of ten minutes. Here's what happens if you calculate the numbers. That ten minutes a day/fifty minutes a week/two thousand six-hundred minutes a year or a total of 43 hours during the year equals more than one week's work. That is the time stolen from your employer.

Five minutes doesn't seem like much until you consider the multiplied effect. Additionally, if you cause fellow employees to "steal time," then you are contributing to their unfaithful stewardship.

Make a list of the ways in which you can be a better time steward for your employer and increase your favor with God, who is your real Boss.

_____

_____

_____

_____

You steal time from yourself and from others when you don't have a planned schedule for your every day and when you don't have a specific time frame within which to accomplish certain tasks.

If you don't like your job, the best way to get one that you do like is to do the one you already have cheerfully and practice God's principles. You will be amazed how God can change things by applying His Word to your employment situation.

"It has been my observation that most people get ahead during the time others waste."

Henry Ford

WORKING THE WORD TODAY

"Praise the Lord for the job covenant. . .I asked the Lord to increase my income at least $1,600 a month. I received a notice that my income would increase $1,800 [a month]. Thank you for praying."

CHARLIE AND CHRIS, HIXSON, TN

CHAPTER 6

T HE KEY TO YOUR FUTURE IS HIDDEN IN YOUR DAILY ROUTINE

Keep a daily 'To Do' list and establish deadlines.

The Apostle Paul wrote in Philippians 3:13, "**This one thing I do...**". This is a good rule for you to follow as well. YOU should ALWAYS KNOW what you need to do next.

Create a written plan, set priorities and fix a time frame in which to accomplish each item in your plan. For instance:

DAILY GOALS   TIME ALLOTTED

Make copies of this grid and have one available for your use every day. If you don't have access to a copy machine just make your daily time planner on notebook paper. The grid doesn't have to be fancy to be effective.

If you are unable to complete specified tasks during the work day and/or your assigned period of time, it's imperative that you properly communicate to your supervisor the reason why the work will not be finished. Ask him/her if you are missing some time saving steps in accomplishing your tasks. With a proper explanation to your employer he should be able to help you accomplish the task in the time assigned or allow you more time to do the job. Don't just keep getting further and further behind. Proper communication is one of the keys to your advancement.

If your goals are of a personal nature, then it becomes extremely important that they are monitored on a daily basis.

Statistics tell us that the average American sees or hears 560 advertisements in a single day. I'm telling you this to let you know that there are millions of time bandits out there waiting to gobble up your precious time and deny you of your God-given benefits. Without definite time priorities you will allow someone else to set your priorities not only for your day but for your life.

WORKING THE WORD TODAY

"After responding to the... prayer, changes started taking place at work. I have gone from reporting to the Houston Division president to the CFO and CEO of [a national home building firm] where I assist them in special projects. [I'm now] believing for substantial increase in salary."

RHODA, CYPRESS, TX

CHAPTER 7

A SK FOR GOD'S WISDOM IN MAKING DECISIONS

"If you need wisdom—if you want to know what God wants you to do—ask him, and he will gladly tell you. He will not resent your asking."

James 1:5 NLT

All too often, we make employment/business decisions based on what we perceive to be the best deal or offer. The reality is that we need to ask for God's wisdom in EVERY decision that we make.

It's always important to seek God and never make an important decision when you are...

...too angry
...too lonely
...too tired
...too hungry.

--When someone unsympathetic to your cause controls the outcome.

--When you have not considered every consequence of your decision.

--When you have not invested time in prayer to God to ask Him to guard you in making your decision.

Too many people say, "I wish I knew what to do" instead of "Lord, tell me what to do."

Are you facing a decision right now? Then I want you to join me in the following prayer. I want you to be as specific as possible. Look at the prayer before you start praying. You will notice the lines that are drawn. In the space that I've provided, you need to get specific with God. List the areas where you need His wisdom.

Once you've personalized this prayer, then I want you to pray it every day.

"Heavenly Father, in the name of Jesus, I want to praise you that the steps of a good man/woman are ordered by you (Psalm 37:23). I rejoice that you are leading me in the way that I should go and that you're teaching me to profit (Isaiah 48:17).

"Your Word says we have the mind of Christ (I Cor. 2:16), so I'm asking that the mind of Christ function fully and freely within me right now.

"I need Your wisdom (James 1:5). You gave wisdom to Solomon (I Kings 3:5-12) and I know that you're no respecter of persons and what you did for him... you'll do for me (Acts 10:34).

"I need your wisdom in the following situations...

_____

_____

_____

_____

"In the name of Jesus, I pray. Amen."

WORKING THE WORD TODAY

"Thank you for your prayers. We just signed the final papers that ended a $625,000 plus debt. We believed that God would cancel this for us. God moved on our behalf and we did not file bankruptcy. Our debts were cancelled. We are working now on restoring our credit rating. We will continue to work and purchase only what we can pay cash for. Our house and cars are all paid for. Praise the Lord."

KATHRYN, WASKOM, TX

CHAPTER 8

B E HONEST ABOUT YOUR MISTAKES

"He that covereth his sins shall not prosper; but whoso confesseth and forsaketh them shall have mercy."

Proverbs 28:13

Let me say this as simply as I know how. If you mess up, fess up, so you can fix it up. If you make a mistake on the job, find options for correction that will prevent further losses to the company.

Talk to your boss immediately and state what happened without making excuses. I am sure that your boss will appreciate your honesty especially if it's something that could be covered up or blamed on someone else. This is especially true if your mistake is going to make the company or your boss look bad.

You need to point out why you think the mistake happened but whatever you do, don't play the victim. If you don't know why it happened, just say that you don't know and ask your Boss to help you to find the answer.

It is important for you to know that God specializes in turning lemons into lemonade.

The 3M Company is a multi-billion dollar company which at one time exclusively made sandpaper. However, because of a shipment of worthless minerals used in the manufacturing process the company was forced to either go under or make significant changes. The mistake forced them to focus on other products and today they have over 60,000 products.

Our history is filled with success stories of people who messed up only to become even more successful because of how they handled a mistake.

WORKING THE WORD TODAY

"After mailing in my Labor Day prayer request form, the government ended my job. Through much prayer they rehired me and moved me to Florida with a promotion to US Customs. Thank you for your prayers."

THOMAS, MIAMI, FL

CHAPTER 9

B E QUICK TO ASK FOR HELP WHEN NEEDED

"A wise man is strong; yea, a man of knowledge increaseth strength."

Proverbs 24:5

"Where no counsel is, the people fall: but in the multitude of counselors there is safety."

Proverbs 11:14

There are five proven ways to ask for help and get it:

1. Select the right person to ask. There are people who find a real satisfaction in sharing what they know. List the people you would seek for wise counsel.

_____

_____

_____

_____

_____

2. Select the right time to ask. Don't approach someone when they are rushed, anxious or stressed. Be courteous and arrange for a moment of their counsel. Make sure the time is convenient for them.

3. Select the right questions to ask. By doing so you convey to the person that you are seeking them because you believe that their talent will have a specific impact on your need or problem.

29

4. Write down the questions you would ask.

_____

_____

_____

_____

_____

_____

5. When you have succeeded by using their counsel, give them credit for their advice. When the person you approached for advice sees you using what they recommended, it will build your relationship with them while making them even more receptive to share knowledge with you in future situations.

6. Make sure you express your thanks very specifically and let them know they have helped create a change for good in your life. Send them an email or write a thank you note.

Always remember that someone who is capable of greatly blessing you is always observing you.

WORKING THE WORD TODAY

"Due to your prayers on Labor Day I received three job offers. I have started a new position [that allows] us to work on our home based business. It is flexible time. This is God's faithfulness and your prayers of agreement with us."
MICHAEL AND KAREN, OVERLAND PARK, KS

CHAPTER 10

A LWAYS DO MORE THAN IS EXPECTED OF YOU

"And whosoever shall compel thee to go a mile, go with him twain."

Matthew 5:41

"If a man is called to be a street sweeper, he should sweep streets even as Michelangelo painted, or Beethoven composed music, or Shakespeare wrote poetry. He should sweep streets so well that all the hosts of heaven and earth will pause to say, Here lived a great street sweeper who did his job well."

Martin Luther King, Jr.

Doing more than is expected:

1.   Gives your creativity a chance to soar. I read that on a bingo card of ninety numbers, there are approximately 44 million ways to make "Bingo." So it is with life. By doing more you will open new areas of creativity.

2.   Causes those around you to raise their own level of performance.

DETERMINE WHAT YOU REALLY WANT IN A JOB

How much income do you personally feel that you need to

31

consider yourself financially successful? Each of us has different needs. Some have a 3 X 5 dream, some a 5 X 7, others an 8 X 10 while some have 16 X 20 dreams. Each is neither right nor wrong. The key is what you want to accomplish.

Using the lines below, make a specific list of what you want out of a job.

_____

_____

_____

_____

_____

"Give me a stock clerk with a goal and I will give you a man who will make history. Give me a man without a goal and I will give you a stock clerk."

J.C. Penney

WORKING THE WORD TODAY
"Praise the Lord for your prayers on Labor Day. God moved me from a $7 an hour job to $10 an hour."

VICTORIA, SPRING VALLEY, CA

CHAPTER 11

IF HE DID IT FOR ME... HE WILL DO IT FOR YOU

There was a time in my life when I was so broke that if I walked by a bank, the alarms would go off. The bankers knew I didn't have any money in the bank so they figured I must be coming to take some out. I was so broke that when we went to have a family photograph taken and the photographer said "cheese," my kids all rushed to stand in line to get some.

All jokes aside, there was a time when we had one nostril above the troubled financial waters. Every now and then a wave would roll over us and we would struggle for air to breathe. But God moved us to a new level and He'll do the same thing for you.

Early in our marriage I had become fairly successful. But through some carefully planned financial disasters orchestrated by the devil that I lacked the spiritual insight to see at that time, I ended up losing a lot of money and moving in with my parents for three years. Then Bev's parents insisted they lend us enough money (more debt) to put a down payment on our current residence, a double-wide mobile home about a mile off the highway up in a field.

WHERE I WAS...

At the time I was pastor of administration at an Assembly of God Church in Goldsboro, NC. We owed multiple loans because of money borrowed to pay the IRS. We were also paying for every trip my babies made to the doctor including any medicines that were prescribed. All we had was a major medical policy for emergencies and that payment was larger than my house payment. But the devil made sure we could use it when my 2-month-old daughter was diagnosed, first with meningitis and then encephalitis and landed at Duke University Hospital for four days. God miraculously brought her out of intensive care, and because we had some insurance we only ended up adding $13,000 to our bulging debt load. That debt also included whatever was left over from the two latest hospital and doctor bills when the children were born. God saved us money on our last child since she was born rather unexpectedly on the bathroom floor.

I came home from work late one afternoon and my wife met me at the door to say God had spoken to her about increasing our tithe. Being the deep man of God that I was, I looked at my wife and said, "Are you really sure it was Him?" Then, when she told me the amount, it made my teeth chatter even on that warm summer day.

So after the kids went to bed that night, I prayed and asked God what He would have us do. When He gave me the same amount to tithe, I was sure that I was in a bad cell phone area. Surely this number was for somebody else. In my mind, I knew that God knew we didn't have the kind of money He was telling us to give. But at the time, I didn't realize it was God testing my heart and obedience in order to take us to the next level. To be truthful, the test shook me up.

GOD HAD PLANS I DIDN'T KNOW ABOUT

So on the very next Sunday, when Bev was placing our increased tithe along with an offering into the collection plate, I was out in the foyer of our church tending to my administrative duties.

A friend of ours named Steve approached me and started telling how his boss had blessed him that Friday by selling him a Cadillac with less than 12,000 miles for $1,000. It was easily worth about $18,000-$20,000.

I began to praise God for his blessing when Steve looked at me rather seriously and said, "Harold, you know I don't need a car like that Cadillac with the tools I haul around for my job. I need a car like that." Steve was pointing out into the parking lot where sat my "anointed" car, which I affectionately referred to as "The Rocket."

My car was a 1979 Delta 88 Oldsmobile with the ugliest two shades of yellow you have ever seen in your life. But I kept that car washed and vacuumed and it was paid for. I called it "anointed" because every time it rained, my trunk became a swimming pool and at least once a week I had to add a quart of Quaker State 10W 30 motor oil to keep it from smoking.

I said, "Look, Steve, I don't have $1,000 to buy this Cadillac and even if I did, I wouldn't do it because you've got at least an $18,000 blessing here."

Steve looked at me and said, "Harold, I'm not asking you to buy the car; I'm giving it to you." I was stunned. I looked at him in disbelief and again being the mighty man of God that I was, I asked, "Are you sure?" Steve laughed and said, "Harold, that's exactly what I asked God yesterday when He told me to do this! To tell you the truth, before I figured out it was God, I said, "Get thee behind me, Satan, this is my car."

GOD'S PLANS WERE MUCH BIGGER THAN MINE

Three weeks later John Avanzini came to speak at our church. It was about an hour and twenty-minute drive from our church to the

Raleigh/Durham, North Carolina Airport. I went to pick up Brother John driving my new Cadillac.

On the drive home, Brother John started sharing with me the vision God had given him to get the Body of Christ out of debt. As he spoke, God stirred in my spirit ideas to share with him on how he might be more effective in fulfilling that vision. This went on for about an hour.

I remember where we were driving down Highway 70 outside Princeton, North Carolina, when Brother John looked at me and said, "You're the only man in seven years of traveling who ever fully understood what God has called me to do." Obviously, I was blessed to hear that mighty man of God offer me such kind words.

I think my next comment was something profound like, "Do you want to eat barbecue or fried chicken?" I was not looking for anything else. I was just blessed to be able to spend time with this man of God.

Shortly after, Bev and I were asked to have dinner with Brother John and Sister Pat after the service and he offered to move us to Fort Worth, Texas to work for the ministry. I was shocked enough that I told Brother John that I would definitely have to pray about it. Two things immediately came to my mind. First, I didn't want to be a hireling. I wanted to only do what God called me to do. Second, I told Brother John that I lived 15 minutes from my parents and that I was my Mama's favorite child. (He pointed out that I was her only child.)

Brother John told me he was leaving on a 4-5 week trip to Asia and then to England. He told me to give him a call upon his return.

Where was God leading?

Bev and I held this offer in our hearts. We didn't tell a single person, not even members of our family. This was a bold step to be taking but we felt as though God was stirring us to go. So at a Wednesday prayer service about two weeks later, we asked a couple that used to live in Fort Worth to meet us the next night. We wanted to ask them some questions about Fort Worth and to pray about the decision that we needed to make.

As Bev and I told the couple about the job offer from Brother John they began to laugh. I asked them what was so funny and they said something that has stayed with me to this day. They relayed that the night before they had been praying to prepare their hearts to pray with us when God told them, "Harold and Bev are moving to Fort Worth, Texas. He's going to work for John Avanzini where he will be used to teach millions of people how to become debt free."

I looked at Bev and said, "Baby, we're moving to Texas."

I called Brother John on the appointed date and told him that we received a clear word from the Lord that we were to move to Fort Worth and join him in helping the Body of Christ become debt free. He said that in his spirit, he felt that we would be joining him.

Up to that point we had never discussed salary. I can't remember that Bev and I had even thought about what it would be. But that night on the phone, Brother John told me he'd move us to Texas and he gave me the amount of my new salary. Suddenly, we realized that the tithe on this new salary was the exact same amount that nine weeks previously God had told my wife and I to increase our tithe to.

God had perfectly planned the whole thing.

Had that increase been convenient to our flesh? Could we afford that kind of increase? No! I think back now and wonder where I would be if we had not obeyed what God directed. It was a 60% increase in our tithe and we were barely buying groceries at the time.

Through God's direction, I now have my own business in addition to traveling the world teaching people how to get out of debt. Last year I was able to tithe more than my beginning salary with Brother John. I know from experience that there are defining moments where God will speak to you. . .times when He's provoking you to move outside your comfort zone and believe BIG. The key is to be obedient even if you don't recognize His visitation at the moment it comes. He wants to know if He can get finances through you because if He can get finances through you, He can certainly get them to you.

God is no respecter of persons (Acts 10:34). I know this book is not in your hands by accident. As you read each chapter, God will move you outside of your comfort zone. He's going to provoke you to take a step of faith and to begin seeing yourself the way He sees you... in a high-paying position. He wants you funding the end-time harvest of souls and He never asks you to work for minimum wage.

"… for he that cometh to God must believe that he is, and that he is a rewarder of them that diligently seek him."
                                        Hebrews 11:6

CHAPTER 12

GOD HAS A PORTION FOR YOU

God has more than a dead end job for you. He has a generous portion of the good things of this earth set aside for you.

That's right. God has a portion of this world's goods for you. Some people minimize what God has in store for them by saying things like: "I live in a bad part of town; there's nothing here for me." And others ruin their chances of having God's best when doubting themselves by saying, "I didn't get an education, so I'll never do much out there in the world."

> *"Behold that which I have seen: it is good and comely for one... to enjoy the good of all his labour that he taketh under the sun all the days of his life, which God giveth him: for it is his portion. Every man also to whom God hath given riches and wealth, and hath given him power to eat thereof, and to take his portion, and to rejoice in his labour; this is the gift of God."*
>
> *Ecclesiastes 5:18-19*

God's Word says He has a portion of this world's goods out there for you. If you believe this Word from God, He is literally saying there's enough out there for you that you can be rich. Unfortunately, not enough Christians take God at His Word.

Traditional misconceptions hold back many of God's children from receiving their portion.

39

Some people have said to me, "Harold, I don't think you should teach Christians to be rich. I've always been told it's wrong for Christians to become rich." If that were the case, then I couldn't teach the Bible, because it says in Proverbs 10:22, "The blessing of the LORD, it maketh rich, and he addeth no sorrow with it."

The scripture is very clear. It's the blessing that the Lord adds to you that allows you to become rich. What do the blessings do for you? They make you rich. If God is in it, your riches will not bring sorrow.

Losing your job brings sorrow. Living in lack brings sorrow. Just getting by brings sorrow. Not being able to give the way you really want to brings sorrow. All these things bring sorrow to you, your family and those who would benefit from your generosity.

> *"...I am come that they might have life, and that they might have it more abundantly."*
> *John 10:10*

That's why God has a different plan, a better plan for you to have a portion and a HIGH PAYING POSITION.

> *"Every man also to whom God hath given riches and wealth, and hath given him power to eat thereof, and to take his portion, and to rejoice in his labour; this is the gift of God."*
> *Ecclesiastes 5:19*

I like reading verse 19 in the New Living Translation...

"And it is a good thing to receive wealth from God and the good health to enjoy it. To enjoy your work and accept your lot in life—that is indeed a gift from God."

A good job, yes, a high paying position is your portion. I know the government says it's not good for the economy when we have full employment. They say it stimulates inflation. But God says it's your portion to be employed all the time. You don't need any down time or unemployed time. I didn't say you won't have it, but you don't need to have it because God's portion for you is full employment. The Bible doesn't say a weapon won't be formed against you (Isaiah 54:17), but it does say that it cannot prosper!

It's God's gift and He says it again over in 2 Corinthians 8:9.

"For ye know the grace of our Lord Jesus Christ, that, though he was rich, yet for your sakes he became poor, that ye through his poverty might be rich."

This is what this scripture says in language we use today:

"You know how full of love and kindness our Lord Jesus Christ was. Though he was very rich, yet for your sakes he became poor, so that by his poverty he could make you rich."
2 Corinthians 8:9 NLT

God is talking about abundant and overflowing prosperity here and it's for YOU. But when you say that it's God's will that a portion of all the world's wealth be given to everybody, many people think that if everybody has an equal share of the wealth of this world, we would all end up in poverty. Not so.

The problem is not a shortage of wealth. The problem is the wrong crowd has control of the wealth. The takers have it instead of the givers. As long as the takers have it, it's going to look like a shortage. But God literally says there is a portion of this world's goods that He has for YOU.

Unfortunately, that's not the way many of us were taught in our "traditional" churches.

> "Making the word of God of none effect through your tradition..."
>
> *Mark 7:13*

I can't tell you how many sermons I heard as a boy telling me I was a worm and certainly not worthy. It was full of all negative stuff. Hear me; we have to get over this identity crisis. Children of God have a portion set-aside for them.

> "Behold that which I have seen: it is good and comely for one to eat and to drink, and to enjoy the good of all his labour that he taketh under the sun all the days of his life, which God giveth him: for it is his portion. Every man also to whom God hath given riches and wealth, and hath given him power to eat thereof, and to take his portion, and to rejoice in his labour; this is the gift of God."
>
> *Ecclesiastes 5:18,19*

God has a portion for you. He not only has a job; He has a HIGH PAYING POSITION for you, <u>but you've got to put yourself in the position to receive it</u>. You must grasp what I am about to teach you or your job, your finances, and your future will forever be in question.

As you have seen in this book, the Bible has much to say about the laborer and his [her] right to full employment and a high paying position. There is a scriptural way to insulate yourself from the devil's plan to minimize your earning power, and even eliminate your job. It's GOD'S FULL-EMPLOYMENT GUARANTEE.

> *"Behold that which I have seen: it is good and comely for one to eat and drink, and to enjoy the good of all his labour that he taketh under the sun all the days of his life, which God giveth him: for it is his portion."*
>
> *Ecclesiastes 5:18*

There it is in BLACK and WHITE. God says it's your IRREVOCABLE RIGHT to enjoy FULL EMPLOYMENT all the days of your life.

It doesn't matter whether you're a sales representative, an assembly line worker, a corporate executive, a farmer, a barber, a plumber's assistant, a car dealer, a secretary, or even if you own YOUR OWN BUSINESS. God will receive your job as a gift to His Kingdom and allow you to continue operating in it—growing in it—prospering in it. The Bible tells us that God will receive your job as a gift, and return it to you as an instrument of His miracle-working power.

DID YOU GET THAT?

I'm going to repeat this sentence once again and I want you to say it out loud as you read it. **THE BIBLE TELLS US THAT GOD WILL RECEIVE MY JOB AS A GIFT, AND RETURN IT TO ME AS AN INSTRUMENT OF HIS MIRACLE-WORKING POWER.**

Moses gave his job to God and when God gave it back, Moses used it to set the captives free. The shepherd's rod in Moses' hand represented his vocation—for he was a shepherd. Moses handed over his shepherd's rod, his very job to God.

In the 17th verse of Exodus 4, we see that God now has the rod in His hand. He then tells Moses to, "...take this rod in thine hand, wherewith thou shalt do signs."

> *"And Moses took his wife and his sons, and set them upon an ass, and he returned to the land of Egypt: and Moses TOOK THE ROD OF GOD IN HIS HAND"*—
>
> *Exodus 4:20.*

Notice it is with the rod of God that Moses put an end to the unfair labor practices of the government of Egypt. With this same rod, God transferred to the children of Israel the POWER TO GET WEALTH (Deut. 8:18). It was with the same rod that God parted the Red Sea—allowing the children of Israel to continue their journey to the land flowing rich with milk and honey.

<u>Now it's time to give your job to God</u>. When you give it to Him, it will become God's job... anointed by His hand and returned to your stewardship as a vehicle through which God can allow His abundance to flow into your hands. In other words, when God returns your job back to your stewardship, as He returned Moses' rod to him, He returns it with His PROTECTION GUARANTEE for as long as you use it with Biblical principles.

Remember, everyone who entered the promise land had the opportunity to prosper. However, some did and some didn't. Those who took God at His Word prospered. The decision is yours.

<u>I want you to know on the authority of GOD'S WORD that</u>

you can be protected from any downturn in the economy. THE ECONOMY DOESN'T HAVE TO AFFECT YOU IN A NEGATIVE WAY! You have been given the POWER to get wealth. And when the enemy of your success closes one door, your faithfulness to your God-given stewardship will allow God to open another way to get His abundance to you! You have His Word on it!

In the past, the leaders of the Debt Free Army have set aside certain times to pray specifically for Christians to get jobs, find better jobs, receive promotions, raises, or bonuses, favor with supervisors and employers and start businesses of their own. Several of the testimonies have been included in this book.

On these very special occasions, I've seen the supernatural power of God manifested on behalf of believers who were willing to take a step of faith. Throughout the pages of this book, you have seen the testimonies of people, just like you, who were blessed because they took this specific step of faith.

It's your turn to give your job to God. I encourage you to complete the "God's Full Employment Guarantee" reply at the end of this book and return it to me immediately. As you complete the reply, it's imperative that you get specific. When you get specific with God, He can get specific with you.

For instance, whatever you need. . .write it down. If it's a new job, a raise, promotion, favor with a supervisor, benefits, more clients, more sales, your own business, whatever it is... write it down.

I will immediately join you in the prayer of agreement once I receive your GOD'S FULL EMPLOYMENT GUARANTEE reply form.

It's time to STOP letting your circumstances, <u>regardless of what they are</u>, dictate your ability to respond to God's plan for your life.

Please don't be offended by what I'm about to tell you. I feel a very special anointing right now as I tell you that GOD ALWAYS HAS MORE for you!

"He will bless them that fear the LORD, both small and great. The LORD shall increase you more and more, you and your children."

Psalm 115:13,14

It is His will for YOU to increase. Regardless of what your annual salary is, GOD HAS MORE FOR YOU! HE WANTS YOU TO SET THE AMOUNT OF MONEY that you want Him to bless you with! Your decisive ACTION will demonstrate to what degree you can be trusted. It's time for you to demonstrate your trust in Him by taking a STEP OF FAITH.

I challenge you to ACT on His faith within you and make an investment in your financial security by sowing a HIGH PAYING POSITION seed with your reply. How much should you give? That's between you and God. But remember, if you want something you've never had, than you've got to do something you've never done. Give God YOUR BEST, whatever that might be in His sight. That's all He wants.

GOD'S FULL EMPLOYMENT GUARANTEE

Please pray with me for a breakthrough in the following area(s). You may mark as many as you feel led to choose:

☐ I feel I'm ready for the following promotion (be specific).

_____

_____

☐ I am unemployed. I would like to work for:

_____

_____

☐ I really need to earn: $_____ per month.

☐ I would like to have the following benefits:

_____

_____

☐ I would like to have favor with the following supervisor(s):

_____

_____

☐ Please join me in the prayer of agreement for my business. (Include the name of your business.)

_____

_____

☐ I need more customers (clients), greater sales and key employees.

IMPORTANT: I'm encouraging you to sow a very specific seed but you and God decide which one.

☐ $40 One dollar representing each hour of the work week.

☐ $160 One dollar representing each working hour of the month.

☐ $960 One dollar for each working hour for six months.

☐ $1920 One dollar representing each working hour of the year.

☐ $_____ Whatever amount God has led you to sow.

Please Print:

Name _____

Address _____

City _____ State _____ Zip _____

Telephone _____

Email _____

Please detach this page and prayerfully complete it front and back. Then enclose it in the envelope that I've provided along with your God-directed HIGH PAYING POSITION seed gift and mail it today.

I look forward to hearing from you.